Investigate

Push and Pull

Charlotte Guillain

www.raintreepublishers.co.uk
Visit our website to find out
more information about
Raintree books.

To order:

☎ Phone 0845 6044371

▤ Fax +44 (0) 1865 312263

▥ Email myorders@raintreepublishers.co.uk

Customers from outside the UK please telephone +44 1865 312262

Raintree is an imprint of Capstone Global Library Limited,
a company incorporated in England and Wales having its
registered office at 7 Pilgrim Street, London, EC4V 6LB – Registered
company number: 6695582

Text © Capstone Global Library Limited 2008
First published in paperback in 2009
The moral rights of the proprietor have been asserted.

Edited by Sarah Shannon, Catherine Clarke, and Laura Knowles
Designed by Joanna Hinton-Malivoire, Victoria Bevan,
    and Hart McLeod
Picture research by Liz Alexander and Rebecca Sodergren
Production by Duncan Gilbert
Originated by Chroma Graphics (Overseas) Pte. Ltd
Printed and bound in China by Leo Paper Group

ISBN 978 0 431932 79 8 (hardback)
12 11 10 09 08
10 9 8 7 6 5 4 3 2 1

ISBN 978 1 406 24460 1 (paperback)
13 12
10 9 8 7 6 5 4 3 2

British Library Cataloguing in Publication Data
 Guillain, Charlotte
  Push and pull. - (Investigate)

A full catalogue record for this book is available from the
British Library.

Acknowledgements
We would like to thank the following for permission to reproduce
photographs: ©Alamy pp. 23 (Laurent Hamels), 25 (Real World
People), 29 (Hugh Threlfall); ©Corbis pp. 10 (Hubert Stadler), 16
(David Madison), 20 (Image100), 28 (Michael DeYoung), 26, 30;
©DK Images p. 24; ©Getty pp. 8, 30 (Dylan Ellis), 9 (Hepp), 11
(Stephen St. John), 12 (Sylvain Grandadam), 13 (Paul Kennedy),
14 (Alexander Walter), 15 (Ariel Skelley); ©Getty Images p. 7
(PhotoDisc); ©Jupiter Images p. 7, ©Nasa p. 27; ©Photolibrary pp.
4 (Rubberball Productions), 5 (GARDEL Bertrand), 6 (Image100),
18 (George Kannavas), 21 (Radius Images); ©PunchStock p. 17
(Juice Images); ©Science Photo Library p. 22 (LEONARD LESSIN);
©Superstock p. 19.
Cover photograph of kicking a football into a goal reproduced
with permission of ©Alamy (Westend61).
Every effort has been made to contact copyright holders of
material reproduced in this book. Any omissions will be rectified in
subsequent printings if notice is given to the publishers.

Contents

Some words are shown in bold, **like this**. You can find out what they mean by looking in the glossary.

Motion

Everywhere we go things are moving around us. There are cars, buses, and trucks on the road. There are people running, cycling, and jumping. When things move from one place to another, they are in **motion**.

Every motion is started by a **force**. Every motion is stopped by a force. A force is a push or pull that works to make something move.

Pushing and pulling

Movement happens when something is pushed. When you kick a ball you push it forwards. When you push a door it opens. When you walk, run, or jump you are pushing on the ground with your feet.

Movement also happens when something is pulled. When you pull a drawer it opens. You put on your shoes by pulling them.

Q Do you push or pull the things in these pictures?

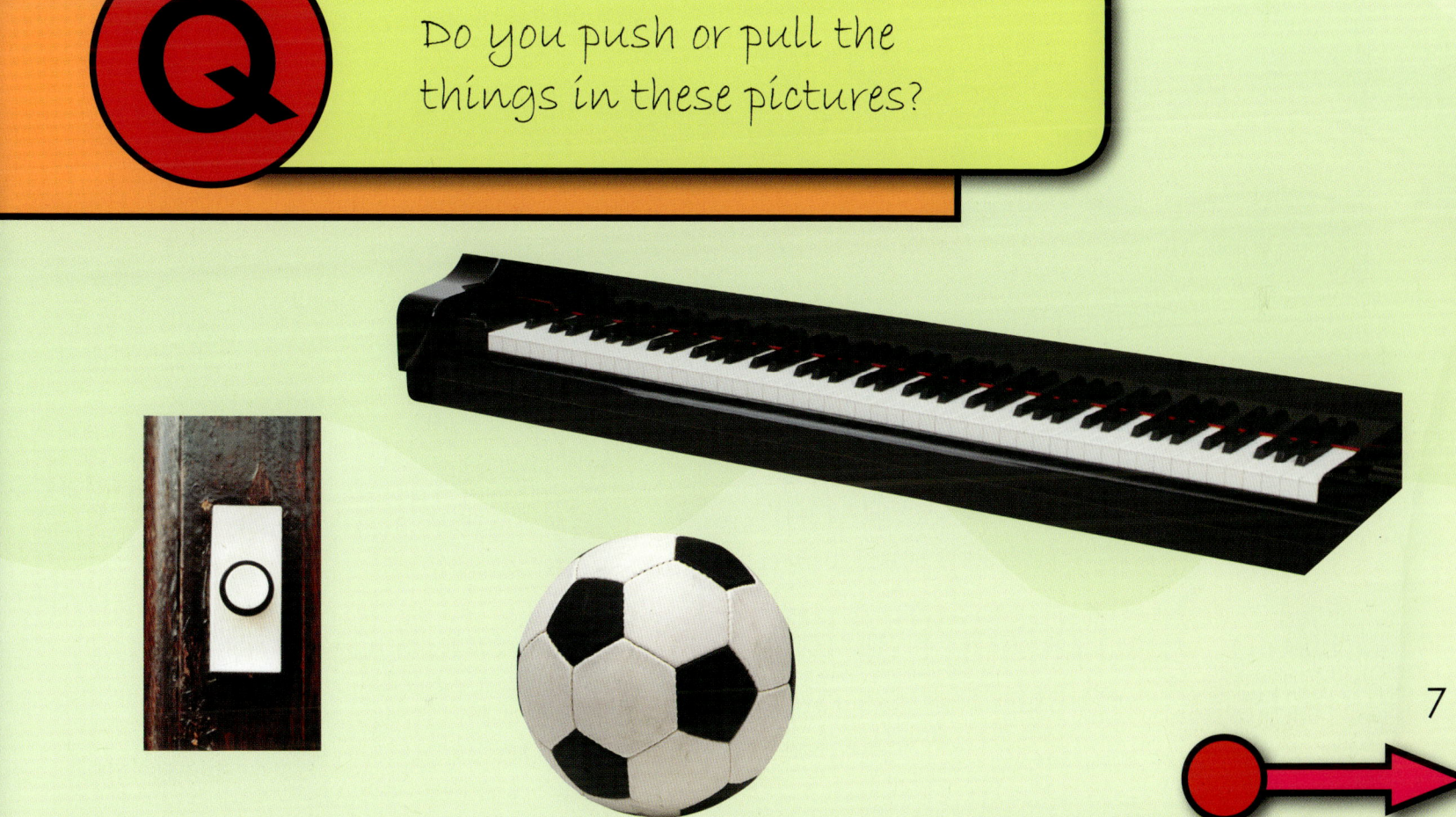

A You move all of the things by pushing them.

Pushing and pulling make **motion** happen. These **forces** can make things move, stop, speed up, slow down, or change direction.

8

Things do not move without pushing and pulling.
Things will stay still if there is no force to move them.

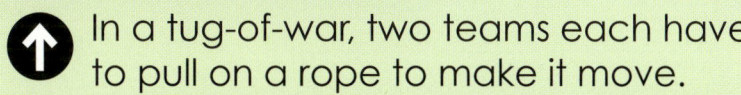
In a tug-of-war, two teams each have
to pull on a rope to make it move.

People can push and pull things. Air or water that
is moving can also push things.

Q How could you push this feather without touching it?

? **CLUE**

• Remember: moving air can push things.

A If you blow at the feather, you make moving air. This will push the feather along.

Moving air, or wind, can also push sailing boats along.

12

The moving water in the sea can push things on to the beach. The moving waves in the sea move surfers through the water.

13

Speed and distance

We push or pull things to make them move.
We can push and pull quickly or slowly.

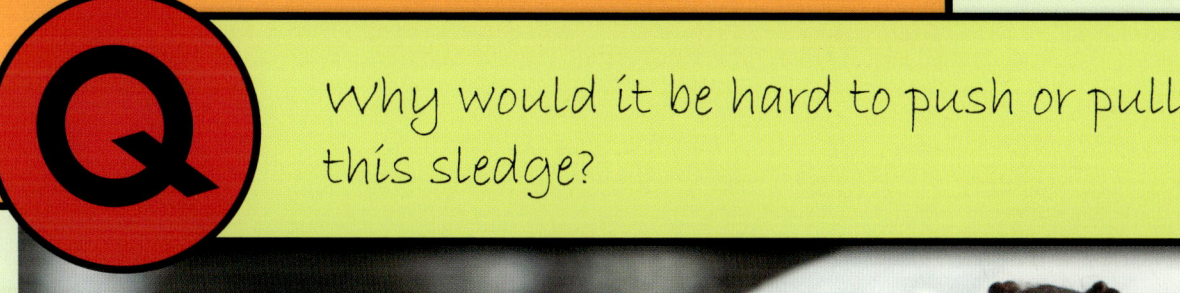

Q Why would it be hard to push or pull this sledge?

? **CLUE**

- How many children are on the sledge?

A It would be hard to move the sledge because it is heavy. Heavy objects need bigger pushes and pulls. It is hard to move heavy things quickly.

Lighter objects need smaller pushes and pulls. They are much easier to move than heavy objects. It is easier to move light things quickly.

When you give something a big push, it can travel a long way. For example, if you kick a football very hard, you are giving it a big push. The ball will travel a long way.

When you give something a small push, it does not travel very far. For example, if you tap a golf ball into a hole, you are giving it a small push. The ball will travel a short distance.

Stopping

We also push and pull things to stop them moving. You grab and pull on a door that is swinging shut to stop it moving. You put out your hand to stop a toy car moving. It is the push of your hand that stops the car.

A player's foot stops the ball by pushing it.

If we give something a big push or pull it will stop moving more quickly. It is harder work to push or pull heavy things to stop them moving.

 Moving things can be dangerous if they are heavy, or moving quickly like this swing.

Springs

A spring is a **coil** of wire. Springs change shape when we push or pull them. We use springs in lots of different ways. There are springs in staplers and some pens. Lots of toys have springs in them.

Q This spring is being pushed together. What will happen when the person lets go?

? CLUE

- The spring will change shape.

A When the person lets go, the spring will move up.

24 When we push a spring down, the spring pushes back up against our hand. When we pull a spring up, the spring pulls on our hand.

spring

Springs help to make things move. When a spring has been pushed down it will always push back up. This **motion** can be used to move objects. Springs can be used in clocks, toys, and other machines to make them move.

25

Gravity

Gravity is the **force** that pulls everything to the centre of Earth. If you drop a ball gravity will pull it down to the ground. The pull of gravity holds us on Earth's surface. Without gravity we would float in the air above the ground.

The pull of gravity makes things move downhill.

When **astronauts** travel into outer space, they move away from the centre of Earth. A long way from Earth there is no pull of gravity. Astronauts can float around in outer space.

Checklist

➡ Every **motion** is started by a **force**.

➡ Every motion is stopped by a force.

➡ A force is a push or pull that works to make something move.

➡ Heavy objects need big pushes and pulls to move.

➡ Light objects need small pushes and pulls to move.

➡ The pull of **gravity** holds us on Earth's surface.

Glossary

astronauts scientists who travel into outer space

coil something that has been wound into loops, such as a spring, or a piece of rope

force a push or a pull that makes something move

gravity the force that pulls everything down to the centre of Earth

motion something moving from one place to another. When we walk we are in motion.

Index